Freddie is a drama teacher, actor, director and performing arts school owner. She teaches LAMDA examinations in schools and privately and she is a LAMDA examiner. She studied Drama & Theatre Studies at Royal Holloway, University of London, and Acting at Drama Studio London. She possesses a teaching qualification in Performing Arts. She is also a fully qualified mindfulness teacher.

She lives near Bath with her family.

Dedicated to my husband, Chris, for endless love and support.

Freddie Underwood

# Acting Monologues | A New Collection | Volume I

Female Roles For ages 7 – 17 Years

Austin Macauley Publishers™
LONDON • CAMBRIDGE • NEW YORK • SHARJAH

Copyright © Freddie Underwood 2024

The right of Freddie Underwood to be identified as author of this work has been asserted by the author in accordance with sections 77 and 78 of the Copyright, Designs and Patents Act 1988.

All rights reserved. No part of this publication may be reproduced, stored in a retrieval system, or transmitted in any form or by any means, electronic, mechanical, photocopying, recording, or otherwise, without the prior permission of the publishers.

Any person who commits any unauthorised act in relation to this publication may be liable to criminal prosecution and civil claims for damages.

The story, experiences, and words are the author's alone.

A CIP catalogue record for this title is available from the British Library.

ISBN 9781035834013 (Paperback)
ISBN 9781035834020 (ePub e-book)

www.austinmacauley.co.uk

First Published 2024
Austin Macauley Publishers Ltd®
1 Canada Square
Canary Wharf
London
E14 5AA

Thank you to my family and friends for supporting me on the journey of writing my first book of monologues. It would not have been possible without them taking over my business for three months for me to focus on the project. You know who you are – Chris, Lou, and Hollie.

Thank you to Simon Mawdsley, a wonderful playwright, for taking the time to read some of my monologues and offer invaluable and encouraging advice.

Thank you to my daughter, Gigi, who inspired some of the monologues in this book. Your sense of humour makes me laugh every day.

Thank you to my students at St Mary's Calne, who gave private rehearsals of the monologues for me to witness them in performance. Your positive feedback was motivating.

# Table of Content

**Ages 7–10 Years**     **11**

   *Goodbye Clover*     *13*

   *Pedro the Purple*     *15*

   *Nanny Nap*     *17*

   *The Memory Robe*     *19*

   *Something from Nothing*     *21*

   *Mistress of this House*     *23*

**Ages 10–12 Years**     **25**

   *A Question of Faith*     *27*

   *Dream Impossible*     *29*

   *Mudmaid*     *31*

   *Double Digits*     *33*

   *Most Felt Feeling*     *35*

   *The Gaze*     *37*

   *Jasmine's Story*     *39*

   *Monkey Mind*     *41*

| | |
|---|---|
| *Sarah* | *43* |
| **Ages 12–14 Years** | **45** |
| *Lunchtime Buddy* | *47* |
| *Forgetting to Check* | *50* |
| *Just a Dress* | *52* |
| *The Manipulative State* | *54* |
| *Trying to Meditate* | *56* |
| *Nomansland Common* | *58* |
| *Refugee* | *60* |
| **Ages 14–17 Years** | **63** |
| *Lockdown* | *65* |
| *Speak More Loudly* | *67* |
| *Witch Trial* | *69* |
| *No Quick Fix* | *71* |
| *AYOR* | *73* |
| *Expectation* | *75* |
| *Offshore* | *77* |
| *The Curse?* | *79* |

# Ages 7–10 Years

# Goodbye Clover

*Morgan is going on holiday with their family and saying goodbye to their favourite teddy, Clover, whom Mum has said they must leave behind.*

It's time to go now, Clover. Mum hasn't changed her mind; I can't take you with me. She says you're too big, and one small teddy is enough for going on holiday. I begged her, but she still said no. Will you be okay? It's only for a week, which isn't too long, not really, but I will miss you, Clover.

I'm going to wrap you up in my bed blanket to keep you safe. This is the one that Granny made for me when I was born. It's soft, and if you feel sad, you can wipe your tears on it, and no one will know. (*Wraps Clover in the blanket.*) There. You can sit on my bed, right here, so you can stare out the window. At night, you might see the stars, and I promise, every night, I will look up at the stars and think of you. Do you promise to look at the stars too, Clover? (*Hugs Clover.*)

I know you get scared of the dark, like me, so I'm going to leave my nightlight on for you. Mum says I need to turn it off, but she doesn't get scared, does she? She doesn't understand; grown-ups don't mind the dark, but we do, so I'm leaving it on for you. It can be our little secret.

Mum's calling me, so I've got to go. Goodbye, Clover. You're my lucky teddy. I love you. See you in a week.

# Pedro the Purple

*Sam is outside the toy shop asking their mum if they can go inside to buy a present for their friend, Esme.*

Mum, just give me five minutes in the toy shop to buy a birthday present for Esme. I'll see you back here in five minutes.

Now what does Esme like? She loves witches! Let's take a look. Warty, warty, warty. Oh, this one is nice – no warts, lovely black robes, black hat, with a broomstick. And I do love her hair; there's something about it. Maybe I'll give it a quick stroke.

*(Gasp)* What's going on? What is this? She's growing bigger, and there's smoke everywhere, green and purple sparks, fireworks! *(Screaming, falling backwards.)*

*(Coughing and blowing the smoke away. A real witch stands before them.)* Where did you…how did you…*who* are you?

*(The witch helps Sam up.)*

Thank you. Are you real? I can't believe it. I mean, one minute ago you were a doll, but now you're, well, I'm not sure. *(Listening.)* An evil wizard, called Pedro the Purple, trapped you inside a doll to stop your good magic? Only when someone strokes your hair three times would you be released from the spell? That was me; I stroked your hair!

*(Listens.)* What did you say? He can track you? He'll find you and take me too? *(Listens.)* I can't possibly go with you. My mum, she would be so worried about me. Oh no, what's happening now? Green slime? Spiders and purple smoke! It's closing in on me.

Why are you rubbing your ring? *(Gasps.)* A portal to your world? Where does it go? She's gone through. What should I do? The smoke is getting closer; I must jump. Here goes.

*(Sam jumps through the portal.)*

# Nanny Nap

*The nanny has taken a trip to the beach with the child in their care.*

Nigel, will you please stop hitting me with the spade? We're here now, finally. Isn't this beach beautiful? Very hot, though. Too hot. Let's get you ready for the sea. What? You forgot your bag? I told you, when we were leaving the hotel room, to get your bag. Your swimming trunks were in your bag! You need to take better care of your things, Nigel. Well, I suppose you could go in wearing your underwear. Hang on, you need sun cream. Here we are. Wait, this is deodorant. Who packed deodorant? No, don't go in without—*(Calling after him)* Nigel!

It's so hot! I've got to sit down in the shade. *(Sitting down)* That's better. Okay, this is nice, very relaxing. I'll keep my eyes on Nigel whilst he plays *(yawning)* and just settle back on the warm sand. I hardly slept a wink last night. It really is so warm. *(Eyes start to close for a moment.)*

Ah! Nigel! You did *not* just throw water on me. What did you do that for? I'm soaked through. We are going back to the hotel room this instant!

I was not asleep; I was just resting my eyes. You didn't go to sleep until the early hours, you know. *(Nigel says he will tell his mother.)* You're going to tell your mother? Nigel, I don't think that's a good idea; that's not going to make mummy happy at all. What about we go and get you an ice cream, how does that sound?

Chocolate? One scoop? All right, two then. *(To the seller)* One chocolate ice cream, please, with two scoops. Thank you. Now, hold it tight, and whatever you do, Nigel, don't drop. Please stop hitting me with your spade, Nigel. I told you to hold it tight!

Time to go back to the hotel room for a nap; we both need one.

# The Memory Robe

*Cypress lives with a woman known as their 'aunt'. Every time a visitor comes to the house, they are locked away in a room, but today, to ensure they cannot be heard, the aunt has locked them in the attic.*

Don't lock me in here. The attic frightens me. Please. Please. I'll ask for forgiveness, just let me out.

*(Crumpling to the floor in distress.)* I wish I knew my mother. All I've ever wanted is to know her and not to be an orphan. To be loved like a mother would love me. Not to be locked in the attic every time I do something wrong.

*(There is a tapping noise.)* What's that noise? *(Listens.)* It is the waterpipes, or a trick to frighten me more? *(Hearing it again.)* There it is again. Maybe my aunt is coming up the stairs to let me out!

No, it's coming from inside the room. *(Searches the room and finds a robe.)*

Look at this. How beautiful. This would fetch all the money in the world. *(Checking no one is looking. Puts it on. Goes to a mirror.)*

Oh, this mirror is a bit dusty. *(Coughing.)* That's better. *(Looks.)* I feel strange, like the room is moving in towards me as if I've seen this picture before. But how could that be?

What happened? Something from the past, like a memory. I saw the queen standing next to me, and she looked just like me. I must be imagining things. I'm going to put this back. What's this? A newspaper clipping. On this day ten years ago, the princess was lost, devastating the queen. Ten years! That's how long I've been *here*.

What if? What if this is mine, and I'm the lost princess?

# Something from Nothing

*Nadia speaks to their assistant, then to their TV audience.*

Get that coffee away from my phone – what's Daddy going to say if I break *another* phone? I need you to get Ariane's number for me. I hear she wants to do a collab with me. Yes, me! Moi.

Move! What are you waiting for? Get on with it. I'm about to go on air.

*(Checking herself in the mirror.)*

This outfit is on point. My viewers are going to love it.

*(Freezes, waiting, smiling.)*

Hello and welcome to *Something from Nothing*, where we listen to all your talented voices. But before we welcome our first contestant, let's talk a little about me, your host, Nadia. You know, my childhood was quite deprived. Daddy didn't even let me have my own pony. I had to share one! And when he sent me to boarding school, do you know what kind of tuck box I had? Not Louis Vuitton or Gucci, but a standard issue one – a tough childhood. But through hard work and determination, I became *something from nothing* – and so could you!

But before we hear *your* voices, I think it's time we heard a song from my latest album. Simply call into the show *now* and shout out the song you want to hear.

*(Pause.)* No calls?

Let's give our viewers a little more time; I'm sure we will be flooded with calls.

*(Pause.)* Still nothing?

*(Awkward.)* Well, enough about me, let's cut to our first contestant on *Something from Nothing. (Leads applause)*

Get Daddy on the line right now!

# Mistress of this House

*Greta is a scullery maid in a grand house. The mistress is out of the house, and Greta has been given instructions to clean every room, apart from the mistress's private rooms.*

Spotless! The mistress can't complain that I haven't cleaned everything as thoroughly as she would wish. There's nothing left to clean.

Oh, she left the door to her private chambers open. I'm not allowed to clean in there; I'll just have a quick look.

What beautiful clothes! Look at those furs, velvets, and silks! Maybe I'll just try on one of them. *(Puts on a dress.)*

Her necklace! She never takes this off; I wonder why she's left it here. No one will know if I try it on for a few minutes. *(Puts on the necklace.)* Oh, it's so beautiful. I've never seen a jewel quite like it. *(Looks in the mirror.)* Mistress? Mistress in the mirror? What? But that's me!

*(Servants enter.)*

Oh, I'm sorry; I wasn't doing anything. I know I'm not supposed to be in here. No, I'm not the mistress. I *am* the mistress *(checks the mirror)* of this house. I own everything here.

Would I like anything? Yes, I would! I would like a glass of my finest champagne. *(Drinks.)* I would like to try on more of my jewels, please. Do I have diamond earrings? Good! Then bring them to me. What other diamonds do I have? A tiara! I am very rich, aren't I? *(Puts on the jewels.)*

I'm so hungry. Would I like a chocolate cake? Of course, I would. I would like the biggest in the land. *(Scoffs down the chocolate cake.)* Oh no, I've got it all over my dress. Now it's dirty. *(Claps hands.)* Servants! I would like a bath. Well, of course, I would like the, what was it? Coconut petals and rose bath salts. Oh! Of course, I meant the other way around. I know that!

*(Takes off the necklace.)*

What are you all looking at? Why are you staring? I order you to run my bath! I'm not a scullery maid. *(Looks in the mirror.)* Oh dear, oh no, I'm in trouble.

# Ages 10 –12 Years

# A Question of Faith

*Young Jane Seymour, at home in Wiltshire, speaking to a member of the Royal Household. Shortly after the birth of Princess Mary to King Henry VIII and Katherine of Aragon.*

*(Shyly)* It is an honour to meet you, my lady. *(Bows)* The house talks of nothing else but the birth of the princess. What a blessing for our great king! Everyone rejoices so for our most beloved Queen Catherine. A daughter. Mary. She lives up to her name, I think, as a most wished-for child.

Forgive me for trembling; I am of a timid nature and do not receive many visitors. Never one from the court! It must be dazzling to live and work in the light of such a king as Henry. I am afraid I would be too frightened to go to court. My mother tells me he has a thousand people attending to him. All those people in one place make me feel dizzy.

Truly? A message from the queen herself, for me? *(Goes to take the letter but withdraws hand)* I must tell you I cannot read or write, except my own name. Jane. My mother instructs me in needlework and household management that befits my station. It is not necessary for a girl to learn reading and writing. As such, please would you kindly read the letter out loud?

*(Listens, the queen asks Jane to consider a role as her lady-in-waiting when Jane turns 18.)*

I cannot refuse. It is my duty to serve the queen. Please tell her, when I am of age, I will proudly serve her as lady-in-waiting. I will learn bravery and pray that I live up to this great privilege bestowed upon me. To know that I may even meet Princess Mary seems like a dream.

*(Jane is asked a question by the queen: How would you describe yourself?)*

A question? This must be important. I seek an answer that is true, for I have been taught to always be truthful. You may tell Queen Catherine that I would describe myself as a candle. A sacred candle, as I strive to always find the light amid the dark moments. Yes, the candle is divine. I worship the one and only God. She will be happy to know, I think, that my Catholic faith could never be shaken by anything or anyone.

# Dream Impossible

*The moment an unlikely dream comes true. Set in Antarctica, Frankie is about to take their first steps onto the ice.*

I've started to sweat. The layers I'm wearing are raising my body heat. My boots are heavy. The gloves so thick I can barely move my fingers. But it's time. Finally, the moment has come. Waddling to the door, like a newly hatched penguin unsure of itself, I awkwardly put on my goggles. I wait. I breathe. Ripples of excitement, or nerves, perhaps both, move around my body. This is it. Someone gives the signal. We are ready. Then, the door opens.

Cold. Sudden, and enormous. Like a wave engulfing me. I close my eyes to the immense brightness. I want to see, to soak in every second, but I'm blind, unable to process the change in light. Gradually, I adjust, start to blink, shuffling down the platform until I take my first step onto the ice. Already my fingers tingle with numbness. I can't feel my toes, try to wiggle them. I force myself to focus, to breathe; I can do this.

There. Antarctica. Endless ice in every direction. Against the bluest sky I've ever seen. My ears strain to hear a sound, but there is none. Apart from my steady breathing. I'm in a dream. Or on another planet. A world away from the business of life. How can there be cities and people when Earth holds a place like this?

Pulling myself along the guide ropes, I move away from the platform. The cold creeps into my bones, tensing muscles and sending shoots of pain through my legs. But I continue to move. Recalling the voices who said it wasn't possible. Don't do it. You can't be serious. When I'm about fifty metres from the base, I stop. Imagine a finish line one step ahead of me. Close my eyes. Smile. Then I take the step. I did it.

# Mudmaid

*A mermaid has rescued a man lost at sea. They have been waiting on the shoreline until the man wakes up.*

Steady. You've been unconscious, drifting in the ocean for a long time. Don't try to move yet; your limbs are weak, and it's unlikely you'll be able to stand, so rest a while. There's a fresh water source over there; I've already given you some; you were very dehydrated. When you are feeling stronger, it's only a short distance away; in the meantime, there's a shell next to you with some water in. Take your time. You'll be safe here in the shade; your skin is blistered from the sun. Soon, you can find the help you need.

Yes, *(reluctantly)* yes, I am a mermaid. I have saved your life, so you must now save mine by never telling a soul about me. Do you understand? Do you swear?

I don't look like a mermaid? Have you seen a mermaid, before me? My hair is short because it is always tangled, and my face is grey from the thick mud and sand that floats up from the seabed, years of grains and particles lodging deep into my skin. I use seal skin to cover my torso and arms to keep warm in the freezing oceanic depths. This tail has many stories to tell, scars from shark attacks and too many times being trapped in wrecks of boats. I look like the ocean – dirty, marked, and strong. What did you think mermaids look like?

Venturing to the surface is forbidden, but I am tasked with locating a new home, so you are lucky that I found you. Megaplume activity has disrupted our way of life, but it isn't easy to find a home for our vast numbers; the ocean is constantly shifting and evolving. Land dwellers, like yourself, think you know these waters, feel certain you know this planet's secrets. You are wrong; there is a world beyond your imagination deep below. You, like all those before you and those yet to come, have no idea of what you don't know.

# Double Digits

*Robin is turning 10 today and is about to open their presents with their parents and friends.*

This is the best birthday ever. Is this my last present? I'm so excited. I think I know what it is, and I want to say thank you now. You are the most amazing parents.

Mum, you've done so much cello tape! *(Calling)* Eva, come and look. I told you about this. It's finally here. *(Opens present, noticeable change but trying to stay happy.)* A book! Thank you so much. *(Opening book and turning it over.)* Will you go and find the others, Eva? I'll be in soon.

*(Quietly, to Mum)* Mum, I thought I was getting a phone for my tenth birthday? I'm really embarrassed; I told all my friends I would be getting one today. Please, Mum, you promised last year. I've been waiting for it. *(Near to tears)* Yes, I know all about that; we do online safety stuff at school. I'll be sensible; please, can I have one? But Mum, everyone has one in my year; I'm, like, the only one who doesn't have a phone now. You always say that – what is there to talk about? I'll help more around the house. I'll put my pocket money towards it; Granny's birthday money will pay for it. Please, Mum, they're all in the kitchen waiting for me. *(Mum*

*tells Robin to get back to their friends; they will discuss it later.)*

*(Visibly composing themselves before going into the kitchen.)* What are you talking about? Oh, it's nothing. Mum just forgot to wrap it; I'm getting it later. What? Katie's on TikTok? Let me see. Are you on TikTok, Eva? Yeah, not yet, but I will be. Let's talk about something else. Do you like my presents? Oh, this is a great book I wanted to get, about the future. That's the main girl. She's *(reading the back)* fighting a u-to-pian future. Yeah, I've heard it's like the best book of the year. Do you want to play on my tablet now?

# Most Felt Feeling

*Impatience chairs the weekly meeting of feelings.*

Hurry up and take a seat. I haven't got all day. I'm calling together this weekly meeting of feelings. Excuse me, could you stop talking over me? Fear, will you quit delaying for once in your life and get over here? I'm in charge, and it's time to crack on. Now! Don't tell me to take it easy. Peace, we can't all be as chill as you. I don't care if Excitement is still in the canteen eating Surprise's doughnuts; this meeting is in session.

As you all know, this week's most *felt* feeling was. *I'm waiting.* Correct! Me. Impatience. More hearts have been racing, more palms have been sweating, and more muscles have been tensing than ever! No wisecracks here, please, Pride.

Hearts don't just race when someone's in love, so there!

Let's take a closer look. Who moved my clipboard with the stats? I said, who moved? Oh, thank you. Startled! That was quick of you. Right. Looking at the figures, the top reason for impatience this week is a classic one: people walking too slowly at the supermarket. Like I said, it's a classic. Stop eyerolling please, Disappointment. This is quickly followed by, waiting to be served in restaurants, being on hold on the phone, queuing in traffic, and simply other people saying, *be patient*. There was a spike in children demanding more ice cream due to the intense weather we've been having. I do love a heatwave. Yes, thank you, Anger; I know you *also* had a spike due to the national shortage of household fans this week. Bold move, Anger – we learnt about that at the annual negative feelings convention last year, didn't we?

Shame, what are you looking at? I know you can't bear failure the same as me, so why? Well, well, well, you've finally decided to join us then, Trust? Truth be told, I had forgotten about you. Bottom of the stats list, huh? When are you going to take the hint that no one has time for you? Look, Anxiety can't even be in the same room as you. Anxiety, come back; this meeting is still in session! Why can't I have my moment in the spotlight without it being spoiled? I'll be on top next week; wait and see. I simply can't wait.

# The Gaze

*The aristocrat in the painting realises there may be a world beyond their confined walls.*

Something isn't right.

The alabaster horses at the end of my chaise lounge look grey, not gleaming white. The bronze cherubs don't seem to smile at me sweetly. They look shocked, like something has taken place. Day after day, month after month, year after year, century after century, nothing has happened here. Adopting the same position each day, my gaze wanders to these familiar surroundings.

But today, something is different; I do *feel* different, like something or some*one* is calling to me. A feeling of being watched. Observed.

*(Walks around the chaise lounge.)* Everything looks the same. *(Notices.)* Apart from this. It does look different. Like a tear. Or an opening.

But wait; I can see the outline of a lady. Right there in the space unseen before. Can I trust my eyes? There is art painted on her arms, and she wears clothes that show off her shoulders in the most unladylike manner. She holds to her face what I can only describe as a small machine. Oh! What was that? A bright light has blurred my vision. *(Staggers back to the chaise lounge.)* Who is she? She looks at me so directly and thoughtfully, like she sees straight into my soul. Wait, she is leaving, her gaze drifting to somewhere else.

This means it can only mean, but I don't know how there must be a world beyond these walls.

# Jasmine's Story

*Jasmine is taking part in a documentary about their life and has been asked to speak to the camera about themselves.*

Hello, I'm Jasmine, and I've, um, I've been asked as part of this documentary to first say a few things about myself. So, yeah, I'm Jasmine, and I'm eleven years old. My favourite food is pasta carbonara, and my favourite singer is Taylor Swift; she's amazing. I've always wanted to see the Great Barrier Reef. I don't know why exactly, but it's always been a dream of mine. But most of all, I adore dancing. I've danced since I was two, and my mum says I haven't stopped dancing since. So, I should also tell you that I was diagnosed with a rare form of cancer, called Ewing Sarcoma, when I was nine. The cancer affects my bones, like the tissue around my bones, and because it's very aggressive, it means I won't live a long life. So, yeah.

It is a bit weird, though; I mean, cancer is scary and *(with a smile)* not very nice, but in many ways, the worst thing in my life has given me the best things in my life. Last year, I got to meet my idol, Taylor Swift, after she read about me, and then, can you believe it, flew over here to spend the day with me. She gave me so much stuff, including free tickets to one of her shows – VIP ones – and we've made plans to write a song together, which just blows my mind, and I'm so lucky. Then, in a few months, I'm going to the Young People's Courage Awards, as I've been nominated for an award, and I'll meet so many amazing people and celebrities there; it'll be like a red-carpet event and everything, so I get to dress up and wear make-up. And now I'm doing this documentary, which is going out on the BBC, and I'm so excited about it because I'll be able to raise loads of awareness for this type of cancer and help others through a charity me and my mum are setting up. That's important to me – to help other children and people with cancer. So, yeah, my life's pretty amazing, and I'm very grateful.

Definitely, the worst thing is not being able to dance at the moment. Because of the cancer, I sometimes get these strokes, and the last one I had was really bad. Right now, I'm in this wheelchair, and it's so annoying, as all I want to do is get back to my dancing. But everyone has been really positive, and I'll keep fighting because dance is the best thing in the world, and nothing will stop me from dancing again. So, that's a few things about myself, um, hope that's okay. Oh, would you like to see a video of me dancing before my stroke?

# Monkey Mind

*Monkey Mind speaks to the audience about the right time to take control of a young mind.*

It needs to be now; I can't wait much longer. My feet won't stay still, heart beating fast; it has always been this way with me. I'm easily distracted, scared of the nothingness of now. The worst time for me is dusk, when night starts to draw in, too pent up to hold back. I need my fix, long to swing into that inner world and feed myself on the whirling storm. I won't sleep; I never sleep. Not when jumping is so much fun. Monkeys don't swing nearly as much as they jump.

My troop is strong these days, so many candidates to choose from. This one, right here, is perfect. I've been watching for only a short time – remember, I am quickly distracted – but I know their mind is a place I will thrive. The face gives them away even before I am in, frustration and worry etched in every pore. And they are young – too young to have learnt the steps to control me. I could scramble in without them noticing anything at all. *(Jumps)* And so, just like that, I am in, no resistance.

Easy. See? No time to waste. Waiting doesn't belong to this part of the mind. Action is needed, now. What should it be, fight, flight, or freeze? Each feeds my fix, so no matter which one to choose. Okay, okay, if I must choose, then flight is the best. Let's pump out some adrenaline; this is going to be fun. Sure, there's no tiger attacking, no critical danger, but there rarely is these days. I'm not waiting, I've already told you. I must make do with the best I can get; in this case, what is it, nothing more than the fear of sleep or trying a new skill. It's funny, really, all those years of evolution, but I've held on, small but mighty. Now sit back and watch the show.

# Sarah

*Set in Victorian times, in a hospital for orphans, Sarah stands up to Nurse Bertha about the cruel treatment and beating of her friend, Clara, for writing a thank you letter to a girl over the wall who gave them apples.*

Stop! Please stop. You're hurting her.

*(Bravely)* I said stop. Look at Clara's hands. The birch is blistering her skin.

She is not wicked. She's just a girl, scared and in pain. Being beaten by an adult. You, Nurse Bertha, you are the one who is wicked. Wicked and cruel to little children in your care. Listen; you will listen to me. I have found my voice, and you cannot stop me from speaking. It is not right for a teacher to hurt a child. And for what? Is it a crime to write a letter to a friend? A person who has shown kindness towards Clara, maybe the only adult who has ever shown any kindness to her?

No, there is nothing sinful about it. Our friend, she lives beyond the walls of the hospital. She gives us apples. It is a blessing to have such sweetness to eat after stale bread and greasy broth. She is kind. Clara wanted to thank her. But you tore that letter, slicing away another glimpse of kindness until there is none left.

You speak of God, but I do not see him here. He does not live in your starch uniforms, your crooked teeth, and stale breath that you bring so close to our faces. This is not what God wants. Why would he want you to punish Clara simply for writing a letter?

I do not care how you punish me now. You want to break me. You will not succeed. There will never be a time, no matter what you do, that you will see me cry.

*(Holds out her hand to be caned.)*

Do it. Do it, and let all see the wickedness in your heart. Not mine.

# Ages 12–14 Years

# Lunchtime Buddy

*Leo has ASD; his school keeps him in the classroom at lunchtime to manage bullying and his fear of the dining room. Claire is his new lunchtime buddy.*

Hi, Leo. I know Mrs Ferris has already explained why I'm going to sit with you. Lunchtime buddy! You know, it was my idea. I don't think it's fair that you have to be in class on your own at lunch. With only a teacher for company. So, here I am! I'm on the school council now, and I want to take it seriously, you know? One day, I want to be an ambassador for the UN. Do my bit to help the world.

You must be lonely all by yourself. Do you want to talk? That's all right. I'll just sit.

*(Pause)*

By the way, I can't stand the dining hall either. Oh, Mrs Ferris told me it's too noisy for you in there. Stinks too. And since they changed the menu, I'm sticking to packed lunches. There is no way I'm eating the slop they call casserole.

What are you reading? Comic strips? I *love* comic strips. Which one is it? *Peanuts* is a classic. You know, for all my talk, I often feel a bit like Charlie Brown. A bit, you know, unsure of myself. But then Charlie had a solid group of friends, and I…

*(Considering)*

Can I ask you something? Like, in a kind way? Why do you tap, like that? Tell me to mind my own business if you like. *(Leo asks what that means. Another child said that to him.)*

Oscar told you to mind your own business? Yeah, that sounds like something Oscar would say. He told me to *go do one* yesterday. I only asked if he was going to recycle his yoghurt pot. Do his bit for the environment. *(Go do one what? asks Leo.)* Go do one? He meant to get lost, I suppose. I *was* in a bit of a mood at the time, so I did ask him a bit, well, I was grumpy.

You know, I sometimes draw my own comics. For fun. I'm not really an artist, but after I've done my homework, sometimes I play around. I'll show you. Once I have my characters stick people. I told you my drawing wasn't great; I'll do speech bubbles, like this, for what my characters say. But when my characters have thoughts, I'll do bubbles like this, because that's what they say in their heads. You see? Let's imagine that this is Oscar, so in his speech bubble we'll put: *Mind your own business*. Let's say this one is you. Can you write in it what you said to him? *(Leos writes; she reads.)* I'm wearing Minecraft pants; what are you wearing? Oh. *(Smiles)* That's quite funny, Leo, but it's quite a personal question. Tell you what, can you write in this bubble what you felt after Oscar said mind your own business? *(He writes.)* I'm confused; okay, I'll write what Oscar might have thought. *(She writes.)* I'm embarrassed. I guess we should consider how our words will affect the other person. *(Thinking)* Like when I ordered Oscar to recycle his yoghurt pot, I was bossy. *(Hears the bell)* There's the bell. You know, this has been fun.

Shall I see you tomorrow at lunchtime? I could tell you all about becoming a UN ambassador.

# Forgetting to Check

*Charlie was killed while crossing a road without checking the traffic. Now a ghost, Charlie addresses their friend, Andi, who, it turns out, is the only person who can see Charlie.*

Andi? I know you can't see me, but I want to talk to you. I miss you, Andi.

You *can* see me? Oh, Andi, can you *really* see me? It's okay; it's a shock for me too. You have no idea how happy this makes me. Yes, yes, I know I'm dead, but I'm here. I don't know how or why, but I'm here, and you can see me, and I've never been so happy about something in all my life. Well, since my dead life, I suppose.

I don't know; it all happened so quickly. We were arguing, weren't we? And then I was running. Didn't see the road, and it just happened. One minute, I was alive, and within seconds, I wasn't alive. Andi, it's not your fault; it's mine. All mine. I shouldn't have run across the road like that. It was stupid of me. I always check; why didn't I check?

Nothing changed; I didn't feel anything. After the car hit me, I stood up, even brushed myself off, like I'd simply fallen over in the dirt. Except, I realised no one could see me; they were all looking down at the road with ashen faces, some with tears in their eyes, and then I looked down and saw.

No one else can see me. Only you. Not my mum, my dad, my other friends. Just you. I mean, I'm over the moon you can; I wouldn't change it for the world now that I'm like this, but what does it mean? Andi, what do I do?

Do you remember when we were little and we used to play hopscotch in the playground? We used to shout at the older kids because they kept pushing us over the squares, Andi, I feel like I'm trapped within the squares of that hopscotch game. It was one moment, just one moment, that I forgot to check. Is this what it's going to be like for me now, forever?

*(Reflecting.)* It's precious, you know, life. I didn't realise. I wish I had thought about it more, wish I'd been more aware of what I had.

# Just a Dress

*The morning after prom, Bobbie speaks to their friend, Sasha, about the night and how amazing it was. Then Bobbie checks their social media, and everything changes.*

It was such a good night. I am shattered now, but it was worth it. Even though I can barely keep my eyes open this morning, I reckon our prom was the best night of my life. Look at these blisters. What time did we stop dancing? It must have been well into the early hours; that band was insane. A rite of passage for all of us. Like our first official steps towards the rest of our lives. *(Pause, yawns)* Yeah, I'll have a coffee, thanks; I'm just going to check my social media.

*(Starts checking her social media and visibly changes as she looks.)* What on earth? Sasha, you've got to see this; I'm not imagining this, right? I know I'm tired, but there are literally hundreds of comments on my Twitter post from last night. *(Laughs)* This is crazy. I don't know; I'll have a look. *(Starts to read)* Sasha, this is bad. Someone has accused me of *cultural appropriation*. What is that? They've quote-tweeted me saying, 'Your stupid prom dress is NOT my culture.' *(Starts getting upset)* Sasha, someone else has called me racist. Oh my god, what is going on? Sasha, I'm not racist; why would they say that? Look at this one; they're saying I'm

just as bad as the bullies at their school who attack them for wearing the outfit I had on. *(Quoting)* 'When an entitled white girl wears the dress, you're disrespecting a whole history of minority suffering.' *(Starts to cry)* Is this real, Sasha? I didn't mean any harm by wearing my dress; I just found it in that lovely little vintage shop on Saffron Road. It was so pretty and unusual, I couldn't resist it. I didn't mean any harm. Everyone last night said I looked amazing; no one said anything like this.

There are so many retweets; how can that be? This isn't going viral, is it? No, I can't put my phone down; check yours, see what else you can find. *(Reading)* This isn't a debate, Sasha; this is nasty. People are accusing me of the worst things. I'm not those things, am I, Sasha? It was just a dress.

*(Her phone pings.)* It's a message from Jade; she asks if I've seen this and why I haven't commented back on any of it. Is that what I should do? Should I make a statement or something, say none of it is true? SASHA, WHAT DO I DO?

Someone's calling me. Hello? *(Answering phone and listening)* Yes, that's me. What? *(To Sasha)* It's a television company asking me if I want to make a comment. How did they get my number? *(Turning the phone off, in shock as she sits down)* This is the worst day of my life.

# The Manipulative State

*Set in a futuristic world, Politiores Onyx speaks to the people of Karus at the trial of a Jupitarean man who is accused of stealing Our Queen: The Pearl's soul.*

People of Karus, my name is Politiores Onyx, and I am delighted to be the adjudicator in this most delicate of matters. Two full red moons ago, this Jupitarean worker sitting in the clutches of fate did willingly steal Our Queen: The Pearl's soul for his own glutinous good. He remains silent; however, we have gathered some valuable information. With your permission, Head of State, I would like to share with the people of Karus my findings. Thank you. To my right is a live link tracking the whereabouts of Our Queen: The Pearl's soulless body. As you can see, all life has been drained from her, because of this man. Yet, it is impossible to try and retrieve her body; the link suggests that she has passed Venus 2981.4 and is heading towards the Sun. As for her soul, it has been crushed, smelted into the brightest crystal in the world, ready to be sold on. This man has blackmailed the state to give up our love for you in exchange for Our Queen: The Pearl's safe return. We do not know if this man's vile words speak the truth or if in fact he is bluffing. Which I believe he is. I implore you, people of Karus, to think what this man deserves, think what he has done to our shining goddess, think about what the state should do. We are intelligent, creative, gifted individuals, and we must stand together and put an end to these anomalies, who think differently and act wrongly. In my opinion, this man's depraved, diabolical, despicable actions towards the state, Our Queen: The Pearl, and you, people of Karus, means that he should be banished to Pluto 1313 and be chased by a madman for all of eternity. We, the state, want to protect you, nurture you, and care for you. Evil does not even come close to what this man is. It is up to you, every one of you, to think: What is justice? Pray for Our Queen: The Pearl, and remember, speak the truth of what is right.

# Trying to Meditate

*A young adult is attempting to meditate as a way to manage their stress.*

Right then, step one, adopt a comfortable seated position, on the floor. Okay *(looking around)*, a comfortable...*(Sits on the floor and tries several ways to sit comfortably: kneeling, legs out front, until finally settling on cross-legged.)* I wouldn't describe it as comfortable exactly, but this will do. Step two, take deep breaths, in through the nose, out through the mouth. *(Breathing in and out.)* My nose is blocked. This is like trying to breathe through the eye of a needle. *(Tries to clear nose, ends up coughing.)* I never knew breathing could result in so much phlegm. Okay, focus. In through the nose *(sniffs)*. In through the nose *(sniffs again, wipes nose)*. In through the nose. Let's move onto step three. I'll do this step, then have a coffee. Step three, focus on emptying your mind. That's simple, surely. I can do that. Empty my mind. Empty my mind. *Empty* my mind. I've got an itch. Come on now, let's start at the beginning. Step one, I'm in a comfortable seated position, well, to a degree I am. Step two, I'm attempting to take deep breaths through my inefficient nose. Step three, I am emptying my mind. Everything is emptying. This is ridiculous; surely, it is psychologically impossible to empty your mind when you have a to-do list that never ends. My never-ending story. This. That. Go there. Do this. Do that. The kids. The housework. The shopping. The home learning. After-school clubs. Dinners. Bath time. Bedtime. Then, repeat. And repeat again. You look stressed, Mindy said. Try meditation, Mindy said. It'll help you unwind, Mindy said. Well, Mindy, I'd rather have a coffee. *(Pause, thinking)* I'll give it one more go. Step one. *(Settles down again)* Step two. *(Breathes)* Step three. *(Goes still silence until she hears her phone ringing).* What is that? *(Picks up phone)* I don't believe it. *(Answering phone)* Mindy, I'm trying to meditate! Yes, right this minute. I was in the middle of emptying my mind, and you called. Uh-huh. Absolutely. I'll be there in ten. A cappuccino with an extra shot, please.

# Nomansland Common

*Inspired by the legend of Katherine Ferrers (it is told she was a highwaywoman by night and a lady of fortune in daytime) who stopped and stole from carriages along Nomansland Common, a remote part of Hertfordshire, in the 1600s. She eventually died of gunshot wounds sustained during a robbery.*

(*To the driver*) Stand and deliver! Easy now; I'm armed. Let go of the reins and make your way down from the carriage, slowly. That's it. Now, kneel. Put your hands behind your head. Good. It's risky business travelling at night in such remote parts. Your cargo must be important. (*Knocking on the side of the coach*) Hands in the air! Open up. Steady, I'm armed. (*The carriage door is opened.*) Out, all of you.

My, my, this is a lucrative sight. Three pretty maidens travelling alone. With no protection, save a lowly coach driver? This is Nomansland Common, ladies, rife with wicked highwaymen lying in wait for easy targets like yourselves. You deduce correctly, mistress; I am no man. I may wear a mask and a three-cornered hat, but no doubt my voice and my figure give me away. In fact, by day, I wear pretty clothes like yourself, and servants address me by a title I will not name, so you are in safer company than most. Now, hand over your jewels and money.

You ask why I should do this? Is there no other reason but survival? *(Laughs)* You have provided me with ample loot tonight, so you will receive my story in return – abridged, of course – I cannot disclose too many details. Kneel! *(Takes a seat)* Upon the deaths of my grandfather, father and brother, my mother fought to name me heiress of a very large fortune. You may be surprised, but she succeeded. I was only a child, but I was rich, in my own right. But when my dear mother died, my stepfather couldn't resist the opportunity to dwindle my fortune away from me by forcing me to marry his nephew, who took possession of all my assets. And there you have it: an orphan with a mission. I had no say in my wealth being taken away, and neither do you. If my stepfather can lawfully take what is mine, then I will *unlawfully* take from others. Now I will be leaving you; my horse awaits. Goodnight, ladies, and Godspeed.

*(A soldier appears from behind the carriage, also armed.)* Yield! Well, well, not so unprotected as I thought. Think carefully, sir; this cannot end peacefully if you make a hasty choice. No violence needs to be committed tonight. Lower your weapon, and I will leave you safely in charge of these ladies. *(A shot is fired; she darts out of the way.)*

# Refugee

*A young person speaks to the audience about life as a refugee in England.*

*(A very long pause – studying the audience)* This. Right now. Ten minutes ago. All this morning. Most of yesterday. Every moment since I stepped off the boat into this country. Eyes. Your eyes, their eyes, too many eyes, watching me. Like *I'm* the danger. There was unimaginable danger in my country. Not here, though. I sense it. The peace, the serenity in the air. If it weren't for all the eyes, I'd be grateful. Maybe quell the fears from my mind. This is what we came here for – the chance to live, undisturbed. An understatement, but what word describes that horror?

I do love my country. This is the difficulty. Yesterday, my father – he had to leave. I am trying to forgive him for the journey he forced upon us. He had little choice in the how. Try as I might to remember, my mind only recalls snatches of the details. The boat already felt like it was sinking when only half of us were in it. Grey water filling my shoes, waves crashing against the side of my body. I kept hearing screams, but I don't know if they were mine or someone else's. Then, finally, the grey shore. With respect, this is a grey country. Or maybe just the little I have seen. It is true I have not gone far yet. This accommodation block is all I have known for three weeks: a grey building, facing another grey building, fenced in by a grey wall, framed by a grey sky. *(Remembering)* Orange. The lifejackets were orange. Like the sun.

Father says they've threatened to arrest him or send us to a safe country. But I thought it was safe here, I told him. He smiled, said not to worry. He smiles so much now. I had forgotten how his eyes come alive when he smiles. I decided not to ask him any more questions. I asked the girl next door to us how long she had been here. She said seven months. According to her, others have waited longer. Maybe in seven months, the sky won't be so grey? Today, I was shouted at by a group outside. They said *immigrant* like it was a bad word. Strange. We call ourselves refugees.

## Ages 14–17 Years

# Lockdown

*Ada speaks to the audience as she casts shadows over the wall with her hands. Ada is in lockdown with a group of school friends in remote France. They were on their way home from a school residential when the lockdown was initiated. The last adult with them, Mrs West, has just died.*

I know you're waiting for it to start. What do you want to see? More shadows? *(She gingerly casts her fingers across her.)* My mum always told me that imagination is the most powerful tool of all. You know, to fill the boredom of a day. I used to just play on my phone. Like any normal teenager would. But my phone's dead now, so I tend to fill my time better than most here. I guess you taught me well, Mum.

My parents, I don't know where they are. At home, I hope. Mum's probably sleeping in my bed right now. She always does that when I'm away; she says the pillow smells like me. Dad? He's probably fixing a shelf or something. He won't be sitting around; maybe that's where I get it from. The need to keep going, keep doing.

Today was a bad day, for all of us. Mrs West – Olivia – she, well, there's no other word for it, she's dead. Never seen someone die before. I thought maybe I would know. I mean, see the moment she passed, or something. But nothing happened; she just stopped breathing, and that was it. I thought I might glimpse a piece of her soul. But it was all so normal. One minute, she was breathing; the next minute, she wasn't. Then we carried her body out to the barn. There was nowhere else to put it. Mia and I, we, covered her in some old blankets; there wasn't really anything else we could do. Tomorrow, we bury her.

So, it's just us now. I mean, Mrs West – Olivia – she was the last adult here with us. It'll be strange without her, you know. I can't shake the feeling that things are going to change now. I mean, they *might* change. Something's in the air, but we must wait. It's all we do; just wait. Wait for the lockdown to end. To return home, safe.

When we first came here – I mean, when they first told us we'd have to stay until everything was safe again – we kept a log of all the different days. I can't even remember who was doing it. I'll show you. Here, look. After this last one, we just stopped. Which seems stupid now because no one knows how long we've been here. My guess is a month. Huh, seems short, right? One month. Twenty-eight days. Don't ask me how many hours.

# Speak More Loudly

*Tiger speaks to the audience about their feeling of anxiety.*

I'm standing by a river in a town whose name I do not know. The moon is full and high. The water looks dark and thick. Like it holds hundreds of secrets. It's still. I could reach down and lift its surface like a box, revealing the past. If I focussed, I could name you ten sounds I hear. The rustling of the leaves in the breeze. An insect of some kind. A dry stick snapping. Is that someone shouting in the distance? A helicopter somewhere in the sky. The sound of my jeans against my skin. My heartbeat. Okay, well, maybe not ten things.

It helps my anxiety. When I stop and focus, I can quiet the voices in my head for a bit. Some days, there's nothing to do but think. I'm not good on those days. The helter-skelter days, I call them. Once I'm spiralling down, the momentum is impossible to stop. If I hold onto the edges hard enough, I can stop the fall for a while, but it's hard. It takes a lot of strength, and the voice likes to tell me I'm not strong enough.

I don't speak much because others speak more loudly. And what is there to talk about? It wasn't long before I felt completely alone. My friends. They are here, but I am alone. Some days, I don't care at all. Some, I care too much. But to be honest, most days I just don't know what is happening to me.

There was one day. My thoughts were scattering in my mind, like cars speeding past on the motorway. Thoughts so fast, I was sick. I found a knife. Traced the blade over my skin. My thigh. My arms. It would be so easy. A release. To silence the thoughts and feel the pain. *(Pause.)* I took a breath. Put down the knife. Not today.

It does feel good, though. To talk. To you. It gives me some clarity. Today is a good day. But tomorrow always comes, doesn't it? And that's what I'm most scared of.

# Witch Trial

*Ginger, a village healer, is accused of witchcraft, killing their sister and has been condemned to burn at the stake. Ginger speaks their final words in the hope of being freed and confirmed innocent of the crimes.*

Mother! Father! Help me! Where are you?

It wasn't me. No! No! Please don't do this. Don't burn me. I'm innocent. I'm innocent. I'm innocent.

You think I killed my sister? I loved my sister. We used to dance and sing, and do everything together. She was the kindest, most gentle person in the world. Why would I kill her? Everyone here knows the closeness of our relationship. We were happy.

I don't *know* who murdered her, but they are the ones who should be punished. They have found the Devil, and the Devil lives in them. I know my sins, and so does God. The kingdom of Heaven waits for me.

You say that I'm a murderer, but that's not the real reason for tying me to this stake. You think I am a witch. A witch, that's right. And because you believe I am evil, you are using my sister's death against me. I didn't do it. I did not murder her. I am not a witch. I am a healer. I am good. *(She breaks down.)*

*(Recovering her strength)* You are threatened by me. A community run by men, and it is those men who want to burn me. They want to burn my power, my strength, as they cannot understand my skill. Know this – my skill is for everyone; it has no threat to your supremacy. Believe me. *They* are the manipulators; *they* are the liars. You may burn me, but your *problem* will not end with me. Healers will get stronger; *women* will become stronger.

I have said enough. I am innocent. I will soon be with my sister.

# No Quick Fix

*A teenager speaks to their dad about bullying at school and their wish to be accepted for who they are.*

I am not considered normal, Dad. This isn't something you can fix, like changing the lightbulbs or sorting out the faulty boiler. You can't make this right, no matter how heroic you are. I really appreciate how you've tried, how you've fought for me in your own way, but there's no magic wand, Dad; the school investigation will change nothing. Come on, those girls – they've been doing their worst for years to anyone who is – *different*. Please let me stay at home for a bit. Mum said she would help me with home-schooling. I can't face another day of it. Give me some time, please, Dad. No more fixing.

*(Dad sits, saying it's time for him to listen.)*

The girls at school, they knew it, maybe even before I did; at least they sensed it. I thought if I kept my hood pulled all the way up, no one would notice me. Keep my head down, isolated, quiet, but they were always there. No, nothing physical, Dad. Anything like that, I'd defend myself. I'm not weak. Remember who beat who in our last arm wrestling battle? They taunt me. They say things, using words loud enough for the whole corridor to hear, so that all eyes fall on me, studying me, like I'm a lab rat, either in sympathy or judgement. Dad, you said you would listen. That's just it, Dad. The things they say, they're true. Dad, stop. They're true. You need to accept it. Because I know you sense it too.

*(Cautiously)* I'm different from who you see me as. I'm not the person you picture in your mind when you proudly boast about my past achievements as a little girl to your friends. I'm not. Inside, I'm not. Inside, I'm trapped, Dad. I want to be me. But I can't express it properly because I feel ashamed. You, Mum, the school, you all want me to fit into a nice little box with the perfect ribbon wrapped around it. No one really wants to look inside the box; the outside is too pretty. There's nothing to be sorry for, Dad; you're listening, and that's what counts. At school, they don't bully me because I'm different; it's because I'm scared. Too scared to open the box, so they taunt me, make me ashamed. Then it gets harder and harder, and I don't know what to do. If I could bring the inside out, be accepted, then it would be a start, wouldn't it?

# AYOR

*Marley speaks to the audience about their disappointing dating life.*

*(To the audience)* I've never had a boyfriend. Or a girlfriend. Never. No hint of romance, no first kiss, not even a corny chat-up line. I mean, there are people in my life. It's not like I live on planet hermit. I have friends that are boys and girls, so, seriously why have I never been asked out?

Don't judge, but I did the thing you should never do: I asked Google. Well, specifically, I went on Yesichat.com, and in a moment of total insanity, I posted the following *(reading online): I've never had a boyfriend or girlfriend. Would you assume that there is something bad or wrong with that person that makes people not want to go out with them? I think it's because I am ugly. I am not fat, however. What is wrong with me?*

I mean, firstly, what is up with my grammar? I suppose there was the small matter of crying like a baby at the time, which may have affected my literary skills. Secondly, how in the world did I, *for a second*, think any response to that would be anything but lunacy? Here you go. So, the first comment from username *IWon'tMurderYou* says, *No one likes a fat girl.* Charming. Clearly, *IWon'tMurderYou* has their own problems with finding a date. That comment was quickly followed by another from *HairyPoppins*, who says, and I quote, *IMO IDK TBF DKDC.* They truly take abbreviations to a whole new philosophical level. I turned the laptop off shortly after that.

The point is, asking online is not the most sensible choice. So, I asked my best friend about her *impressively active* dating life. I mean, she's gorgeous, so it totally makes sense. Tall, slim, dark, she's a perfect mix of Amazonian beauty mixed with Kardashian glamour. Plus, she's smart, funny, and sweet. Maybe I should be dating *her*? Way too complicated and definitely in the friend-only zone. Even asking her was a dead end; I mean, it's too easy for her. Suitors just fall into her path wherever she goes. Like in some Bridgerton-inspired belle of the ball series.

But she did give me a number. A friend of her most recent flame, Josh. *(She experiments with the sound of the name.)* Josh. Josh and Tessa. Tessa and Josh. It grows on you.

Without getting ridiculously ahead of myself, back to the issue at hand, I messaged Josh, and he seems like a great guy. Likes football, debating, is two years older than me, goes to a private school, blah blah. But now he wants me to send a photo.

Which is scary. What do I do? If I send a photo, what sort of photo do I send? I want him to like me.

# Expectation

*Kimberley has been chosen to speak at school speech day. She considers the pressure of education and what it has cost her and her peers.*

Thank you. I'm grateful to be chosen to represent the whole year on this day, our last school speech day. We are about to take our first steps into the world, to shake off the final specks of our adolescence and step into the light of our future adult selves. I am getting philosophical, please forgive me. To those of you who are awaiting final grades, like myself, our futures remain uncertain until we know whether our conditional offers have been accepted. Whether we are deemed worthy enough to enter the great halls of our preferred universities. A *practical* problem that leaves no room for philosophy.

Nevertheless, there are so many achievers in this room. Take a moment to look at the person sitting next to you. They, like you, have worked relentlessly to achieve, through education, acceptably outstanding results in every exam. To better themselves at every possible opportunity, to become someone of note. Or at least on paper. But what has it cost them? What has it cost *you*? We are achievers, but what else are we?

Since I can remember, I have been fed a narrative. Work hard, Kimberley, and all your dreams will come true. But the truth of the matter is that I had no time for dreams. I was too busy working, achieving, to have any time for soft, pillow-coated dreams. And in place of my own dreams, my parents and our teachers were quick to fill in the space. So, to speak the truth, as I await the news of whether I am accepted to study English at UCL, I now ask myself: Is this my dream or someone else's? My parents are happy with my choice, as are my teachers, but am I? As I have come to realise, my lack of dreams was brought about by a lack of time and choice. No time to detour from the path of achievement. No time to consider any other option open to me in life. Any why? The constant, numbing, all-absorbing pressure of expectation. You know this. I see your nods. You recognise it, feel it creeping into you, know it so well you wear it almost like a well-worn jacket despite how it itches and heats you. We are the generation of pressure and expectation, living out the dreams of others. And we are about to take our first steps into the world.

# Offshore

*Set on an oil rig off the coast of Texas in the Gulf of Mexico, Georgie is American and determined to work her way up the ladder of the oil industry.*

Lap it up. I'm looking good, right? It's not every day that this roughneck wears a suit. But Brad, after today, I'm damn sure that I'll be wearing pumps instead of rigger boots. *(See the helicopter in the distance approaching)* Here they come. I reckon I've got about five minutes until they land, so how about we drink in the view together, huh? *(They switch positions and look out to the water.)* Never gets old, this view. Blue as far as the eye can see. Offshore has always been my life, Brad, but I'm hoping to change that today. Sure, I'll miss it; this has been my life for years.

It's no easy feat having ambition in the oil industry, Brad. First woman on this rig to be given an interview for management. I mean, look at them; they're even flying out here to see me. I need this, Brad. The whole industry needs it. They need me. Yes, Brad, exactly because I am a woman. Look around you, where are the women at, Brad? In this world, women represent less than fifteen percent of the workforce; half the guys here could be my grandfathers. In a game of poker, I would be holding all the cards, and you can bet your life I'm going to play them. They wouldn't dare overlook me right now. Not when the papers continue to label us as *dirty*. They are desperate for fresh blood. But I'm not going to make it easy, Brad. Whatever they offer me, it won't be enough. They'll have to pay what I want if they want any kind of meaningful future. Oh, I know it, Brad. I'll get them their financial results, in exchange for being the first woman promoted to the board. Guess the wait worked out well for me, huh? Y'all better move out my way; I'm ready and rarin' to go.

I don't need luck, Brad. Those climate protestors the other week gave me the perfect opportunity. Everybody's so concerned about fossil fuels right now, the company knows it's on its last legs unless they make drastic changes. Cue the lady of the hour. Gonna get over there now, Brad. You better get practising calling me ma'am from now on.

# The Curse?

*Remy speaks to her brother Josh about periods in an attempt to educate him about women and what they go through every month.*

They're called tampons, idiot. I can put my stuff wherever I want; I share this bathroom with you. For crying out loud, I think you can put up with my tampons in here when I have to come into your stench every morning. Oh, are you embarrassed in case one of your bird-brained friends happens to see them, and what, freaks out because they are radioactive? There's no way you are going anywhere; sit down. I mean it, if you want any kind of lasting relationship with a girl, you need some reprogramming. Sit down, Josh!

Listen, I am trying to help you. Maybe help to reduce the moron in you? Well, who else is going to tell you about it? Boys your age have no clue what it's like. Look, I'm going to start with an apology. When your voice broke, I teased you about it; well, you did sound like a tone-deaf frog half the time – I'm sorry – but Josh, your voice breaking, which you made such a fuss over, is nothing in comparison to bleeding every single month of your life, from around age 12 to old lady, or whenever it is women get the menopause. Yeah, every month. Jeez, you really are an idiot.

Okay, I'm sorry.

Seriously, women bleed every month, and these little white tampons have to be stuffed up our vaginas in order to keep the blood from flowing everywhere. I mean, when you really think about it, it's pretty cool that women can literally bleed for five days without dying. And honestly, Josh, it does feel like I'm dying some months, because of the cramps.

Cramps?

Well, they can be a sort of dull ache, right here, but like all the time. Then some days, it's like an intense pressure in there that feels like your body is squeezing out your lower intestines with a plunger. Josh, you've gone a bit pale. Deep breaths, Josh, you can listen to this without puking, I promise you. Get over it.

*(He apologises.)* I'm sorry too. I'm your sister, and I need you to be grown up about this. Do some research and look at how the male gaze objectifies women in the way it wants, but all the other parts of being a woman that terrify men – like periods – have made us feel ashamed of what happens to our bodies every month. Don't be part of that, Josh. Support me like the amazing brother I know you are. *(He asks what he can do.)* Well, to start with, let's see how amazing you can be right now. How? Pop to the shop and buy me some more tampons, will you? I've got the worst cramps.